# KPIs
## *For* National Judiciary and Security Bodies

AHMED ELY Mustapha

Copyright © 2023 AHMED ELY Mustapha

All rights reserved.

ISBN : 9798399897226

# DEDICATION

Dedicated to the tireless professionals of justice, whose unwavering belief in the power of justice inspires them to seek more tools for its fulfillment.

KPIS FOR NATIONAL JUDICIARY AND SECURITY BODIES

# CONTENTS

Introduction ..................................................................................2

1 Planning strategy ......................................................................5

2 Planning strategy map ..............................................................7

3 kpis presentation ......................................................................9

4 kpis in planning strategy .........................................................11

5 kpis in public administration ...................................................14

6 kpis in security sector .............................................................18

7 kpis in judiciary sector ............................................................21

8 kpis in terrorism approach ......................................................24

9 kpis : general difficulties .........................................................27

10 kpis : difficulties in security sector ........................................30

11 kpis difficulties in judicial sector ...........................................33

12 kpis: effectiveness criminal chain .........................................36

Conclusion ................................................................................40

## ACKNOWLEDGMENTS

I would like to express my gratitude to my dedicated colleagues who have shown support and attention towards my project of writing this book

# INTRODUCTION

Planning is a crucial process that helps individuals, organizations, and institutions achieve their goals effectively. It involves establishing objectives, determining the actions required to achieve those objectives, and allocating resources accordingly. Planning provides a roadmap for decision-making, resource allocation, and implementation of activities to attain desired outcomes. It is a dynamic and iterative process that allows for adjustments and adaptations as circumstances change.

Planning strategy refers to the approach or framework used to develop and implement plans effectively. It involves considering various factors such as organizational objectives, available resources, external environment, and stakeholders' expectations. A well-defined planning strategy provides direction, clarity, and coherence to the planning process. It helps in setting priorities, identifying potential risks and opportunities, and aligning efforts towards the desired outcomes.

Contribution of Key Performance Indicators (KPIs) to Planning Strategy:
Key Performance Indicators (KPIs) are measurable metrics that indicate the performance and progress towards specific objectives or goals. They play a vital role in planning strategy

by providing quantitative and qualitative insights into the effectiveness and efficiency of actions taken.

KPIs contribute to planning strategy in several ways. Firstly, they provide a means to assess the current performance and identify areas for improvement. By tracking relevant KPIs, planners can evaluate the success of previous initiatives and make data-driven decisions for future planning. This iterative approach allows for continuous learning and optimization.

Secondly, KPIs facilitate effective resource allocation. By monitoring KPIs, planners can identify resource gaps or excesses and adjust allocations accordingly. This ensures optimal utilization of resources and helps avoid unnecessary expenditures.

Furthermore, KPIs enable benchmarking and comparison against industry standards or best practices. By establishing relevant KPIs and tracking performance against them, organizations and institutions can assess their relative position, identify competitive advantages or weaknesses, and make informed decisions to improve their standing.

Contribution of KPIs to National Judiciary and Security Bodies Planning Strategy:
In the context of national judiciary and security bodies, planning strategy becomes even more critical due to the high stakes involved in maintaining law and order and ensuring the justice system's integrity. KPIs play a crucial role in shaping the planning strategy of these institutions.

For national judiciary bodies, KPIs can help assess the efficiency and effectiveness of court processes, case disposition rates, and backlog management. By tracking KPIs related to case clearance rates, trial durations, and judicial workload, planners can identify bottlenecks and implement strategies to improve the efficiency of judicial proceedings.

Similarly, for security bodies, KPIs contribute to planning strategies by providing insights into crime rates, response times, crime-solving rates, and public satisfaction with security services. Monitoring these KPIs enables planners to identify emerging trends, allocate resources strategically, and develop proactive measures to address security challenges.

Moreover, KPIs related to the performance of specific units or departments within these bodies can aid in identifying areas of strength and areas needing improvement. This information can guide training programs, resource allocation, and the development of specialized units to enhance overall effectiveness.

KPIs play a vital role in planning strategy by providing measurable insights into performance, enabling resource optimization, facilitating benchmarking, and guiding decision-making. For national judiciary and security bodies, KPIs are invaluable tools for assessing and improving efficiency, effectiveness, and public trust in their operations.

# 1 PLANNING STRATEGY

A planning strategy refers to the approach or methods used to create and implement a plan of action. It involves identifying goals, objectives, and tactics to achieve them, as well as allocating resources and assessing risks and potential challenges. A good planning strategy should be flexible, adaptable, and able to adjust as circumstances change. Some common elements of a planning strategy include:

1. Setting clear and specific goals: Identifying what needs to be achieved and how it will be measured.
2. Developing a timeline: Establishing a timeframe for when goals will be achieved and creating a schedule of activities.
3. Identifying resources: Assessing what resources are needed to achieve the goals and how they will be acquired.
4. Assessing risks and potential challenges: Identifying what could go wrong and developing a plan to mitigate these risks.
5. Communicating the plan: Ensuring that everyone involved in the plan is aware of their roles and responsibilities.
6. Monitoring and evaluating progress: Regularly reviewing the plan and adjusting as needed.
7. Being adaptable: Being willing to change the plan as

circumstances change.

Overall, a planning strategy is a crucial step in achieving success in any project or initiative. By taking the time to carefully plan and strategize, organizations can increase their chances of success and minimize the likelihood of failure.

# 2 PLANNING STRATEGY MAP

A strategy map is a visual representation of an organization's strategic plan, outlining the key objectives, initiatives, and performance measures that will be used to achieve the overall goals and objectives of the organization. It typically includes four main components:

1. Financial Perspective: This section focuses on the financial objectives of the organization, such as increasing revenue, profitability, and shareholder value.
2. Customer Perspective: This section focuses on the organization's customer-related objectives, such as improving customer satisfaction, loyalty, and retention.
3. Internal Process Perspective: This section focuses on the organization's internal processes, such as improving efficiency, quality, and productivity.
4. Learning and Growth Perspective: This section focuses on the organization's human capital and organizational capabilities, such as developing and retaining employees, and fostering a culture of innovation and continuous improvement.

The strategy map is often used as a tool for communicating and aligning the organization's strategic plan with all employees, as well as for monitoring and measuring progress towards the achievement of the organization's goals and objectives.

# 3 KPIS PRESENTATION

A KPI (Key Performance Indicator) presentation is a visual representation of a company's performance and progress towards achieving its goals and objectives. It typically includes a variety of charts, graphs, and tables that display data and metrics relevant to the company's performance.

The purpose of a KPI presentation is to provide a clear and concise overview of a company's performance and progress, and to identify areas for improvement and growth. It is typically used by management and stakeholders to track and evaluate the company's performance, and to make data-driven decisions.

A typical KPI presentation may include the following elements:

1. Executive Summary: A brief overview of the company's performance and progress.
2. Goals and Objectives: A list of the company's goals and objectives, and how they align with the company's overall strategy.
3. Metrics and Data: Charts, graphs, and tables that display data and metrics relevant to the company's performance. This may include financial metrics, customer metrics, employee metrics, and operational metrics.
4. Analysis and Insights: An analysis of the data and metrics, and insights into the company's performance and progress.

5. Recommendations and Action Plan: Recommendations for improving the company's performance, and a plan for implementing these recommendations.

6. Conclusion: A summary of the company's performance and progress, and a look ahead to future goals and objectives.

A KPI presentation is a valuable tool for companies to track and evaluate their performance and progress, and to make data-driven decisions. It is typically presented to management and stakeholders on a regular basis, such as monthly or quarterly.

# 4 KPIS IN PLANNING STRATEGY

1. Sales growth: Measuring the increase in sales over a specific period of time can help assess the effectiveness of the planning strategy.
2. Market share: Tracking the company's market share compared to competitors can provide insight into how well the planning strategy is working in terms of gaining or maintaining market position.
3. Customer satisfaction: Surveying customers to measure satisfaction with the company's products or services can indicate how well the planning strategy is meeting customer needs.
4. Production efficiency: Measuring factors such as lead time, inventory turnover, and capacity utilization can provide insight into how efficiently the company is producing and delivering products or services.
5. Employee engagement: Surveying employees to gauge engagement and satisfaction can provide insight into how well the planning strategy is aligning with the needs and goals of the workforce.
6. Return on investment (ROI): Tracking the return on investment for specific projects or initiatives can help assess the financial viability of the planning strategy.
7. Resource allocation: Measuring how resources (financial, human, technological) are being allocated and utilized can provide insight into how effectively the company is managing and utilizing resources.

Case on Key Performance Indicators (KPIs) in planning strategy:

**Retail Store Expansion**

A retail company wanted to expand its operations by opening new stores in different locations. To ensure effective planning and monitor the success of the expansion strategy, they identified the following KPIs:

- New Store Openings: Number of new stores opened within a specific time frame.
- Revenue Growth: Percentage increase in overall revenue after store expansions.
- Customer Acquisition: Number of new customers acquired as a result of the expansion.
- Sales per Square Foot: Average sales generated per square foot in the new stores compared to existing ones.

By tracking these KPIs, the company was able to assess the effectiveness of their expansion strategy and make informed decisions for future planning.

**Digital Marketing Campaign**

An e-commerce company launched a new digital marketing campaign to drive online sales. To measure the success of the campaign and optimize their marketing strategy, they focused on the following KPIs:

- Conversion Rate: Percentage of website visitors who made a purchase.
- Cost per Acquisition: Average cost incurred to acquire a new customer.

- Return on Ad Spend (ROAS): Revenue generated per dollar spent on advertising.
- Customer Lifetime Value (CLV): Predicted value of a customer over their lifetime.

By closely monitoring these KPIs, the company was able to identify areas for improvement, allocate marketing budgets effectively, and refine their overall planning strategy.

**Supply Chain Optimization**

A manufacturing company aimed to optimize its supply chain to reduce costs and improve efficiency. They established the following KPIs:

- Inventory Turnover: Number of times inventory is sold and replaced within a given period.
- Order Fulfillment Time: Average time taken to fulfill customer orders.
- Supplier Performance: Percentage of on-time deliveries from suppliers.
- Overall Equipment Effectiveness (OEE): Efficiency of manufacturing equipment.

By tracking these KPIs, the company could identify bottlenecks, streamline processes, and make data-driven decisions to enhance their supply chain planning strategy.

# 5 KPIS IN PUBLIC ADMINISTRATION

1. Service delivery efficiency: measuring the speed and effectiveness of government services such as issuing licenses, permits, and approvals.
2. Transparency and accountability: monitoring the level of transparency and accountability in government operations and decision-making.
3. Citizen satisfaction: measuring the level of satisfaction among citizens with the services and policies provided by the government.
4. Financial management: monitoring the government's financial performance, including budgeting, spending, and revenue collection.
5. Employee satisfaction: measuring the level of satisfaction among government employees with their work environment and job satisfaction.
6. Crime reduction: measuring the effectiveness of government programs and policies in reducing crime rates in the community.
7. Environmental sustainability: monitoring the government's efforts to promote environmental sustainability, including reducing emissions and waste management.
8. Public health: measuring the effectiveness of government policies and programs in improving public health outcomes, such as reducing infant mortality rates and increasing vaccination coverage.
9. Access to education: monitoring the government's efforts

to improve access to education for all citizens, including increasing enrollment and graduation rates.
10. Economic development: measuring the government's efforts to promote economic development, including job creation and business growth.

Case on KPIs use in public administration:

**Improving Citizen Satisfaction in Government Services.**

A public administration department in a city faced numerous complaints from citizens regarding delays in processing applications for various permits and licenses. To address this issue, they decided to implement key performance indicators (KPIs) to measure and improve their service delivery. They established the following KPIs:

- Application Processing Time: The average time taken to process an application from the date of submission.
- Customer Service Response Time: The average time taken to respond to citizen inquiries and complaints.
- Application Accuracy Rate: The percentage of applications processed without errors or omissions.

By monitoring these KPIs regularly, the department identified bottlenecks in their processes and implemented improvements. They streamlined their application review process, implemented an online application system, and increased staff training. As a result, the application processing time reduced by 30%, customer service response time improved by 40%, and the application accuracy rate increased by 20%. This led to higher citizen satisfaction and improved the overall image of the public administration department.

**Enhancing Transparency and Accountability in Government Procurement**

A national government recognized the need to improve transparency and accountability in its procurement processes. They implemented KPIs to measure the effectiveness of their procurement activities. The KPIs included:

- Procurement Cycle Time: The average time taken to complete a procurement cycle, from the initiation of the procurement process to the contract award.
- Competitive Bidding Rate: The percentage of procurement processes that involved competitive bidding.
- Supplier Performance: The evaluation of suppliers based on their delivery timelines, quality of goods or services, and adherence to contract terms.

Through the monitoring of these KPIs, the government identified areas of improvement. They implemented measures to streamline the procurement cycle, trained procurement officers on best practices, and increased the use of competitive bidding. As a result, the procurement cycle time reduced by 20%, the competitive bidding rate increased by 15%, and supplier performance improved significantly. This not only enhanced transparency and accountability in government procurement but also resulted in cost savings and improved value for money.

## Increasing Employee Productivity and Efficiency in a Government Agency

A government agency was struggling with low employee productivity and efficiency. To address this issue, they introduced KPIs to measure individual and team performance. The KPIs included:

- Output per Employee: The amount of work produced by each employee within a specific timeframe.
- Time Utilization: The percentage of time spent on productive activities versus non-productive activities.

- Quality of Work: Evaluation of the accuracy, completeness, and overall quality of work produced by employees.

By implementing these KPIs, the agency was able to identify areas where employees needed additional training or support. They provided training programs to enhance skills and knowledge, implemented time management strategies, and encouraged a culture of quality and continuous improvement. As a result, the output per employee increased by 25%, time utilization improved by 15%, and the quality of work improved significantly. This led to better service delivery, increased efficiency, and improved overall performance of the government agency.

## 6 KPIS IN SECURITY SECTOR

There are many different KPIs (key performance indicators) that can be used to measure the effectiveness of a security program. Some common KPIs in the security sector include:

1. Security incidents: The number of security incidents that occur within an organization.
2. Compliance: The percentage of compliance with industry regulations and standards.
3. Vulnerability management: The percentage of vulnerabilities that are identified and mitigated within a certain timeframe.
4. Security awareness training: The percentage of employees who have completed security awareness training.
5. Incident response time: The time it takes for an incident to be detected, contained, and resolved.
6. Security audits: The number of security audits that are conducted, and the percentage of non-compliances identified.
7. Risk management: The number of risks identified and mitigated and the percentage of risks that have been mitigated.
8. Cybersecurity maturity: The overall maturity level of the organization's cybersecurity program

It's important to choose the right KPIs for your organization and to track them regularly. This will help you identify areas of improvement, measure progress over time, and demonstrate the value of your security program to stakeholders.

Case on KPIs use in security sector:

### Enhancing Incident Response Time

A security company implemented a key performance indicator (KPI) focused on reducing incident response time. They set a target of responding to security incidents within 15 minutes. To achieve this, they invested in automated incident detection and response tools, improved their communication channels, and provided training to their security personnel. As a result, the company witnessed a significant reduction in incident response time, ensuring that security threats were addressed promptly and efficiently.

### Increasing Physical Security Compliance

A government agency wanted to improve physical security compliance across its facilities. They implemented a KPI to measure the percentage of facilities that met the required security standards. To achieve this, they conducted regular audits, implemented training programs for facility managers, and provided resources to address security gaps. As a result, the agency saw a steady increase in compliance rates, ensuring that all facilities adhered to the necessary security protocols.

### Strengthening Cybersecurity Incident Resolution

A financial institution aimed to enhance its cybersecurity incident resolution process. They implemented a KPI to measure the average time taken to resolve cybersecurity incidents. The target was set at three days. To achieve this, they implemented an incident management system, established clear escalation procedures, and trained their cybersecurity team on incident handling techniques. As a result, the institution witnessed a significant improvement in incident resolution time, minimizing the impact of cybersecurity breaches.

### Improving Employee Security Awareness

An international corporation recognized the importance of employee security awareness in preventing security breaches. They implemented a KPI to measure the percentage of employees who completed mandatory security training. To achieve this, they developed engaging and interactive training modules, introduced incentives for completion, and regularly communicated the importance of security awareness. As a result, the corporation observed a notable increase in employee participation and a higher level of security consciousness across the organization.

### Enhancing Security System Uptime

A technology company relied on a robust security system to protect its sensitive data and infrastructure. They implemented a KPI to measure the uptime of their security system, aiming for 99.9% availability. To achieve this, they conducted regular maintenance, invested in redundant systems, and established a proactive monitoring and response team. As a result, the company experienced minimal downtime, ensuring continuous protection of their assets and reducing the risk of security breaches.

# 7 KPIS IN JUDICIARY SECTOR

1. Case clearance rate: The percentage of cases that have been resolved within a given timeframe.
2. Case backlog: The number of cases that have not been resolved within a given timeframe.
3. Time to disposition: The average time it takes for a case to be resolved.
4. Conviction rate: The percentage of cases that result in a conviction.
5. Recidivism rate: The percentage of individuals who return to the justice system after being released from custody.
6. Jury trial rate: The percentage of cases that go to trial by jury.
7. Satisfaction rate: The percentage of individuals who are satisfied with the outcome of their case.
8. Diversity and inclusion: The percentage of people from diverse backgrounds who are represented in the judiciary system.
9. Access to justice: The percentage of people who have access to legal representation and the court system.
10. Efficiency and productivity: The number of cases handled per judge or court staff member.

Case on KPIs use in judiciary sector:

## Efficiency and effectiveness of court processes

In a judicial system reform initiative, a country's judiciary implemented key performance indicators (KPIs) to measure the efficiency and effectiveness of court processes. One KPI focused on the average time taken for the resolution of civil cases. Before the implementation of KPIs, the average time was around two years. However, after introducing KPIs and implementing various measures such as case management systems and improved court processes, the average time for case resolution reduced to eight months. This led to increased satisfaction among litigants, reduced backlog, and improved access to justice.

## Transparency and accountability

In another jurisdiction, a Supreme Court implemented KPIs to enhance transparency and accountability in the judiciary. One KPI focused on the timely delivery of judgments. Prior to the implementation of KPIs, there were significant delays in delivering judgments, causing frustration among litigants and undermining public trust. After the implementation of KPIs, the Supreme Court established a target of delivering judgments within three months of the completion of hearings. As a result, the court started meeting the target consistently, leading to improved trust in the judiciary, reduced backlog of pending cases, and increased efficiency in the overall judicial process.

## Performance of judicial officers.

A judicial administration body introduced KPIs to improve the performance of its judicial officers. One of the KPIs was the disposal rate of cases by individual judges. The aim was to incentivize judges to work efficiently and reduce the backlog of cases. By regularly monitoring the disposal rate and providing feedback to judges, the administration was able to identify areas where support or additional resources were needed. This approach led to increased productivity and accountability among judges, resulting in a reduction in pending cases and improved overall efficiency in the judicial system.

### Timely access to justice

In a developing country, a judiciary faced challenges in providing timely access to justice, particularly in remote areas. The judicial system implemented KPIs to measure the establishment and functioning of mobile courts in underserved regions. The KPIs included the number of cases heard, the average time taken for case disposal, and the satisfaction level of the litigants. By monitoring these KPIs, the judiciary was able to identify areas where additional resources were required, leading to improved access to justice and reduced disparities in legal services between urban and rural areas.

### Efficiency of court processes

In an effort to enhance the efficiency of court processes, a judiciary implemented KPIs to measure the effectiveness of alternative dispute resolution (ADR) methods. One of the KPIs focused on the settlement rate of cases through ADR mechanisms such as mediation or arbitration. By monitoring the settlement rate and providing training to judges and court staff on ADR techniques, the judiciary saw a significant increase in the utilization of ADR and a corresponding decrease in the burden on traditional court proceedings. This approach not only expedited the resolution of cases but also resulted in cost savings for litigants and improved overall access to justice.

# 8 KPIS IN TERRORISM APPROACH

1. Number of terrorist attacks per year
2. Number of deaths and injuries caused by terrorist attacks
3. Percentage of terrorist attacks that were foiled by security forces
4. Number of terrorist cells or organizations active in a country or region
5. Percentage of terrorist attacks that were motivated by religious or ideological beliefs
6. Number of individuals arrested or detained for terrorism-related activities
7. Number of terrorist-related incidents reported in high-risk areas or cities
8. Number of foreign fighters or extremists returning to a country from conflict zones
9. Number of social media accounts or online platforms used to spread terrorist propaganda
10. Economic impact of terrorist attacks on a country or region, including loss of tourism and investment.

Case on KPIs use in terrorism approach :

**United States Counterterrorism Efforts**

In the wake of the 9/11 attacks, the United States intensified its counterterrorism efforts. The key performance indicators (KPIs) used in measuring the effectiveness of these efforts included:

1. Number of Terrorist Attacks Prevented: The focus was on preventing terrorist attacks within the United States and on American interests abroad.
2. Disruption of Terrorist Networks: The aim was to dismantle and disrupt terrorist networks by capturing or eliminating key leaders and operatives.
3. Reduction in Funding Sources: The goal was to identify and disrupt the financial networks that supported terrorist organizations, reducing their ability to carry out attacks.
4. Enhanced Intelligence Sharing: KPIs included improving coordination and information sharing between various intelligence agencies, both domestically and internationally.
5. Public Confidence and Support: The government aimed to maintain public confidence by effectively communicating counterterrorism efforts and ensuring support from the general population.

## European Union's Counterterrorism Strategy

The European Union (EU) has implemented a comprehensive counterterrorism strategy, focusing on KPIs such as:

1. Strengthened Border Security: KPIs were established to enhance border controls, including improving the effectiveness of identity verification systems and sharing intelligence across member states.
2. Cooperation and Information Sharing: The EU emphasized the importance of cooperation and information sharing among member states, promoting joint investigations and intelligence exchange.
3. Prevention of Radicalization: KPIs were developed to measure efforts in preventing radicalization by implementing programs targeting vulnerable individuals and communities at

risk.

4. Improved Aviation Security: The EU implemented stricter aviation security measures, including enhanced passenger screening and improved cargo security.

5. Disruption of Online Terrorist Propaganda: KPIs included efforts to identify and remove online terrorist propaganda, reducing the ability of extremist groups to spread their messages.

Case Study 3: Kenya's Counterterrorism Measures

Kenya has faced significant terrorist threats, particularly from groups such as Al-Shabaab. Key KPIs in Kenya's counterterrorism efforts include:

1. Prevention of Cross-Border Infiltration: Kenya focused on securing its porous borders, preventing the infiltration of terrorists from neighboring countries.

2. Disruption of Financing Channels: KPIs were established to target and disrupt the financial networks supporting terrorist activities, reducing their capabilities.

3. Enhanced Intelligence and Surveillance: The government aimed to improve intelligence gathering capabilities, including the use of advanced surveillance technologies and collaboration with international partners.

4. Counter-Radicalization Programs: Kenya implemented programs to counter radicalization, focusing on education, community outreach, and rehabilitation of individuals at risk of extremism.

5. Protection of Critical Infrastructure: KPIs included measures to enhance the security of critical infrastructure, such as airports, transportation systems, and government buildings.

# 9 KPIS : GENERAL DIFFICULTIES

1. Data collection and accuracy: Collecting accurate data for KPIs can be a challenging task, particularly for businesses that have multiple departments or operate in different locations.
2. Determining which KPIs to track: Identifying the most important KPIs for a business can be difficult, as there are often many metrics that could be tracked.
3. Keeping up with industry changes: As industries change, so do the KPIs that are most important to track. Businesses must stay up-to-date with industry trends to ensure they are tracking the right KPIs.
4. Managing data overload: With so many metrics to track, it can be easy to become overwhelmed with data. Businesses must be able to effectively manage and analyze large amounts of data in order to make informed decisions.
5. Limited resources: Small businesses may have limited resources and may not be able to invest in advanced data analytics tools and personnel to collect and track KPIs effectively.
6. Difficulty in understanding the results: Even with accurate data, interpreting the results and understanding the implications of different KPIs can be difficult. This can make it challenging to use the data to make informed decisions.

Cases of difficulties encountered:

**KPIs and overall objectives**

Company X is a retail business that operates multiple stores across different locations. They want to improve their overall performance and set key performance indicators (KPIs) to measure their progress. However, they face several general difficulties in defining their KPIs.
Firstly, they struggle with determining the most relevant metrics for their business. With multiple departments and functions, they find it challenging to identify the KPIs that align with their overall objectives. Additionally, they encounter difficulties in collecting and analyzing the necessary data to measure the KPIs accurately. The company lacks a centralized data management system, making it time-consuming and challenging to gather the required information from different sources. Lastly, there is resistance to change within the organization, as employees are accustomed to the existing performance measurement methods. Introducing new KPIs requires a cultural shift and effective communication to ensure everyone understands the purpose and benefits of the new metrics.

**Defining and implementing effective KPIs**

Non-profit Organization Y aims to increase its donor engagement and fundraising efforts. They decide to implement KPIs to monitor their progress. However, they face general difficulties in defining and implementing effective KPIs. Firstly, they struggle with setting measurable goals. As a non-profit organization focused on social impact, quantifying their objectives can be challenging.
They need to find a balance between qualitative and

quantitative indicators to capture the essence of their work accurately. Secondly, they encounter difficulties in tracking and collecting relevant data. The organization relies on multiple platforms and systems for their operations, making it cumbersome to consolidate the necessary data for KPI measurement. Furthermore, they face resistance from staff members who are already overwhelmed with their existing workload. Implementing new KPIs requires proper training and change management strategies to ensure buy-in and successful adoption.

## Developing effective KPIs

Start-up Z is in the technology industry and wants to scale its operations rapidly. They decide to establish KPIs to monitor their growth and performance. However, they face general difficulties in developing effective KPIs. Firstly, they lack historical data to establish baseline measurements and benchmarks. As a start-up, they have limited historical performance data, making it challenging to set realistic targets and track progress accurately. Secondly, they struggle with aligning KPIs with their ever-changing business goals and strategies. Start-up Z operates in a highly dynamic market, and their objectives frequently evolve. It becomes crucial to regularly review and update their KPIs to ensure relevance. Lastly, they face resource constraints, particularly in terms of data analytics capabilities. Limited resources make it difficult to implement sophisticated data tracking and analysis systems, hindering their ability to measure KPIs effectively.

# 10 KPIS : DIFFICULTIES IN SECURITY SECTOR

1. Lack of standardization: There is a lack of standardization in the security sector, which makes it difficult to measure and compare performance across different organizations and regions.
2. Limited data availability: Many security organizations struggle with collecting and analyzing data to track performance and identify areas for improvement.
3. Complexity of security threats: Security threats are constantly evolving and becoming more complex, making it difficult to accurately measure the effectiveness of security measures.
4. Difficulty in measuring intangible outcomes: Security is often focused on preventing negative outcomes, such as crime or terrorist attacks, which can be difficult to measure in terms of tangible results.
5. Balancing competing priorities: Security organizations must balance competing priorities such as protecting citizens, preserving civil liberties, and maintaining operational efficiency, which can make it difficult to establish clear performance metrics.
6. Limited resources: Security organizations often have limited resources, making it difficult to invest in the technology and personnel needed to effectively track and measure

performance.

7. Difficulty in measuring the effectiveness of preventative measures: Many security measures are designed to prevent negative outcomes, which can be difficult to measure in terms of tangible results.

Cases of difficulties encountered:

### Defining and measuring Key Performance Indicators

In the security sector, a major difficulty in defining and measuring Key Performance Indicators (KPIs) arises from the dynamic and evolving nature of security threats. For instance, a security agency implemented KPIs to measure the effectiveness of their counterterrorism efforts. However, they faced challenges in accurately quantifying the reduction in the overall threat level due to the emergence of new, unpredictable terror groups. This made it difficult to establish meaningful KPIs that would reflect the actual impact of their security measures.

### Lack of a standardized framework

A security company responsible for safeguarding a high-profile event encountered difficulties in determining relevant KPIs due to the lack of a standardized framework. They faced challenges in aligning their security goals with measurable indicators, as there was no universally accepted set of KPIs for the security sector. This hindered their ability to assess the effectiveness of their security operations and make data-driven decisions to improve their services.

### Quantifying accurate indicators

In the cybersecurity domain, an organization struggled to identify suitable KPIs to measure their information security posture. They faced difficulties in defining and quantifying indicators that accurately reflected the level of protection against cyber threats. This was primarily because the rapidly evolving threat landscape required constant adjustment of KPIs, and existing metrics failed to capture the organization's preparedness against emerging cyber risks.

## Data collection and analysis

A law enforcement agency aimed to assess the efficiency and effectiveness of their crime prevention initiatives through KPIs. However, they encountered difficulties in data collection and analysis. Due to the fragmented nature of criminal activities and varying reporting practices across different jurisdictions, obtaining accurate and reliable data for measuring KPIs proved challenging. This limited their ability to assess the impact of their efforts and make informed decisions on resource allocation.

## Meaningful benchmarks and performance metrics

A security service provider faced difficulties in setting realistic KPI targets for their personnel due to the inherent unpredictability of security incidents. Despite their best efforts, they struggled to establish meaningful benchmarks and performance metrics. The dynamic nature of security incidents and the complex environment in which their staff operated made it challenging to develop KPIs that accurately reflected individual and team performance, hindering effective evaluation and improvement of their security services.

# 11 KPIS DIFFICULTIES IN JUDICIAL SECTOR

1. Case backlog: The number of pending cases in the court system can be a major difficulty in the judicial sector. This can lead to delays in the resolution of cases, which can be frustrating for both victims and defendants.
2. Case disposition time: The time it takes for a case to be resolved can also be a difficulty in the judicial sector. This can be due to delays caused by a lack of resources, such as too few judges or court staff, or due to the complexity of the case.
3. Case dismissal rate: The rate at which cases are dismissed can be a difficulty in the judicial sector. This can be due to a lack of evidence, lack of jurisdiction, or other legal reasons.
4. Case appeal rate: The rate at which cases are appealed can be a difficulty in the judicial sector. This can be due to dissatisfaction with the outcome of the case, or due to a lack of legal representation.
5. Case conviction rate: The rate at which cases result in a conviction can be a difficulty in the judicial sector. This can be due to a lack of evidence, lack of witnesses, or other legal reasons.
6. Courtroom capacity: The capacity of courtrooms can be a difficulty in the judicial sector. This can be due to a lack of funding for court facilities, or due to a lack of court staff.
7. Court technology: The use of technology in courtrooms can be a difficulty in the judicial sector. This can be due to a lack of

resources for technology, or due to a lack of training for court staff.

Cases of difficulties encountered:

### Inefficient Case Management System

In a certain judicial sector, the lack of a modern and efficient case management system posed significant challenges in measuring and tracking key performance indicators (KPIs). The existing system relied heavily on manual processes, leading to delays, errors, and difficulties in retrieving accurate data. As a result, it became extremely challenging to assess the productivity, timeliness, and efficiency of the judiciary.

Without a proper case management system, it was difficult to measure important KPIs such as case disposition rates, average case processing time, and backlog reduction efforts. The lack of real-time data and reporting capabilities made it impossible to track progress accurately, hindering the identification of areas that required improvement. Consequently, stakeholders faced difficulties in making informed decisions and implementing effective strategies to enhance judicial performance.

### Insufficient Resources and Staffing

In another jurisdiction, the judicial sector grappled with KPI difficulties due to insufficient resources and staffing. The court system experienced a significant backlog of cases, leading to delays in case resolution and increasing pressure on the judges and supporting staff.

Due to the lack of adequate resources, courts struggled to meet KPIs related to case disposition rates and case processing time. Additionally, the shortage of judges and support staff hindered the timely scheduling of hearings, resulting in delays and an overwhelming workload.

Moreover, the limited resources posed challenges in implementing effective training programs for court personnel, affecting the quality of services provided. The lack of staff development opportunities contributed to difficulties in achieving KPIs related to judicial competence and performance.

**Inadequate Performance Measurement Framework**

In a particular judicial sector, the absence of a comprehensive performance measurement framework led to difficulties in defining and tracking KPIs effectively. The lack of clear and standardized metrics made it challenging to evaluate the performance of judges, court staff, and the overall judicial system.

Without a robust measurement framework, it was difficult to assess KPIs such as case resolution rates, customer satisfaction, and compliance with judicial standards. The absence of a consistent methodology for data collection and analysis resulted in inconsistent reporting, making it challenging to compare performance across different courts and jurisdictions.

Furthermore, the absence of a performance measurement framework limited the ability to identify best practices, areas of improvement, and allocate resources strategically. It hindered the development of targeted interventions to address challenges and enhance the overall performance of the judicial sector.

## 12 KPIS: EFFECTIVENESS CRIMINAL CHAIN

The effectiveness of criminal justice systems can be measured by a variety of KPIs. Some of the most important ones are: arrest rate, conviction rate, recidivism rate, time to conviction, case clearance rate, victim satisfaction, officer satisfaction, and community trust.

1. Arrest rate: The percentage of individuals arrested in relation to the total number of crimes committed.
2. Conviction rate: The percentage of individuals convicted in relation to the total number of arrests made.
3. Recidivism rate: The percentage of individuals who re-offend after being released from prison or completing a sentence.
4. Time to conviction: The average length of time it takes for a case to go from arrest to conviction.
5. Case clearance rate: The percentage of crimes that are solved and cleared by arrest or otherwise.
6. Victim satisfaction: The level of satisfaction expressed by victims of crime regarding the criminal justice process.
7. Officer satisfaction: The level of satisfaction expressed by

law enforcement officers regarding their job performance.
8. Community trust: The level of trust and confidence expressed by members of the community regarding the criminal justice system

Cases of difficulties encountered:

## Lack of Standardized KPIs in a Law Enforcement Agency

In a law enforcement agency, the lack of standardized key performance indicators (KPIs) created difficulties in measuring the effectiveness of the criminal chain. Different departments within the agency had different KPIs, leading to inconsistent tracking and evaluation processes.

For example, the investigations department focused on the number of cases closed, while the intelligence department measured success based on the quantity of actionable intelligence gathered. The lack of alignment in KPIs hindered collaboration and coordination between these departments, resulting in inefficiencies and gaps in the criminal chain.

Without standardized KPIs, it became challenging to assess the effectiveness of the overall criminal chain. The agency struggled to identify bottlenecks, measure the impact of various interventions, and allocate resources optimally. This lack of clarity in measuring performance hindered the agency's ability to improve its effectiveness in tackling crime.

## Data Quality Issues Affecting KPIs in a Prosecution System

In a prosecution system, difficulties arose in effectively measuring KPIs due to data quality issues. The system relied on accurate and timely data to track the progression of criminal cases through the various stages of the legal process.

However, inconsistencies and errors in data entry and management compromised the reliability of KPI measurements.

For instance, incorrect case status updates, missing or incomplete information, and inconsistent categorization of offenses created challenges in assessing the effectiveness of the criminal chain. KPIs such as average case resolution time, conviction rates, and case backlog became unreliable indicators due to data quality issues.

The lack of reliable KPIs hampered decision-making processes within the prosecution system. It was difficult to identify areas of improvement, allocate resources effectively, and measure the impact of policy changes or process enhancements. The system struggled to assess its performance accurately and identify opportunities for efficiency gains.

## Inadequate Technology Infrastructure for KPI Monitoring in a Corrections System

In a corrections system, the lack of adequate technology infrastructure posed difficulties in monitoring KPIs for the effectiveness of the criminal chain. The system relied on manual processes and outdated systems, making it challenging to collect and analyze data in real-time.

For example, tracking recidivism rates, inmate population trends, and staff performance required manual data entry and extensive paperwork. The absence of automated systems and integrated databases hindered the timely and accurate measurement of KPIs.

The lack of technology-driven KPI monitoring affected decision-making within the corrections system. Without real-time data and analytics, it was challenging to identify areas for improvement, allocate resources efficiently, and address emerging issues promptly. The system struggled to measure its effectiveness accurately and lacked the agility needed to respond to evolving challenges.

These case studies highlight some of the difficulties faced in measuring the effectiveness of the criminal chain due to issues with standardized KPIs, data quality, and technology infrastructure. Addressing these challenges is crucial for improving the overall effectiveness of the criminal justice system.

# CONCLUSION

In conclusion, this book has delved into the crucial topic of Key Performance Indicators (KPIs) in the context of national judiciary and security bodies. Throughout its pages, it has provided a comprehensive panorama of useful KPIs and highlighted their significant role in this domain.

The book has demonstrated that KPIs serve as invaluable tools for assessing the effectiveness, efficiency, and overall performance of national judiciary and security bodies. By setting clear and measurable targets, these indicators enable decision-makers to evaluate and monitor progress, identify areas for improvement, and make data-driven decisions.

Moreover, the book has shed light on various categories of KPIs that are particularly relevant in the realm of national judiciary and security. It has explored KPIs related to case management, court efficiency, crime prevention, public safety, and resource allocation, among others. By understanding these different metrics, stakeholders can gain insights into the strengths and weaknesses of their systems, leading to more informed strategies and policies.

Furthermore, the book has emphasized the importance of aligning KPIs with the overarching goals and objectives of national judiciary and security bodies. It has highlighted the significance of tailoring indicators to specific contexts and considering the unique challenges faced by these institutions. By customizing KPIs to reflect the particular needs and priorities of each organization, it becomes possible to track progress effectively and drive meaningful change.

Additionally, the book has stressed the need for continuous evaluation and refinement of KPIs. It has recognized that the landscape of national judiciary and security is dynamic and constantly evolving, necessitating the adaptation of KPIs to changing circumstances. Regularly reviewing and updating indicators ensures their relevance and reliability in measuring performance and achieving desired outcomes.

This book has provided a panoramic view of useful indicators, their application, and their significance in this domain. By embracing KPIs as an integral part of decision-making and performance management processes, national judiciary and security bodies can enhance their effectiveness, promote accountability, and ultimately contribute to a safer and more just society.

## ABOUT THE AUTHOR

AHMED ELY Mustapha PhD, CSP, CEH. Criminal chain practitioner and trainer, the author is a Certified Strategy Specialist in the judiciary and security reform projects in Africa and MENA region.

www.ingramcontent.com/pod-product-compliance
Lightning Source LLC
Chambersburg PA
CBHW070137230526
45472CB00004B/1566